Sister,

Set Yourself

FREE

by

Decembre Pierce

1663 LIBERTY DRIVE, SUITE 200
BLOOMINGTON, INDIANA 47403
(800) 839-8640
WWW.AUTHORHOUSE.COM

First published by AuthorHouse 07/29/05

ISBN: 1-4208-6593-5 (sc)

Printed in the United States of America
Bloomington, Indiana

This book is printed on acid-free paper.

Acknowledgements

I would like to acknowledge several special people that were very instrumental in the mental preparation, planning and writing of this book. These people have helped me to become the woman that I am today.

Thank you all for caring about both my mental and physical well-being and for always believing in me:

- Mr. Eston Baker
- Attorney Rosiland Grant
- Mr. Jean Drake and Dr. Fredrick Mercilliott
- Pastor Shirley Johnson
- Attorney Louie Wilson
- Reverend Franklin Williams

Thank you all for all the moral support!

Finally, for always standing by me whether I was right or wrong, for forever believing in my abilities to succeed in all that I do, for never giving up on me and for always telling me the truth whether I wanted to hear it or not, **my friend and confidant** Dr. Cosmo Kenton. **Thank You!**

Dedication

There were so many things and so many people that inspired me to write this book and I am grateful to them all. When people said that I couldn't make it in life and that I couldn't write a book, I became destined to prove them wrong. I am the WOMAN that I am today because of those people.

There are several people that I would like to Thank. First, I thank my ex-husband who taught me that no matter how good of a wife you are, to some people that still isn't good enough. Thank you to that ex-lover/ex-boyfriend who taught me that you can't give everyone your heart. Thank you to that ex-friend/ex-roommate who taught me that you can't befriend or trust everybody in life, and thank you to everyone that said that I would never succeed in life. All of you have taught me valuable lessons in life that I will never forget!

With forever endearing love, this book is for the people that I am truly thankful to with all my heart: My mother Mollie, whom without her, I would not be alive today. **I LOVE YOU** and **I THANK GOD** that you are my mom. My sister Laticiama, who is the best sister that God could have ever given me. You have supported me when no one else did and you have believed in me when others didn't. I am so grateful every day that I have you for my sister. **I LOVE YOU** and remember our favorite line from our favorite movie, "Nothing but death can keep me from you"! (Color Purple) To my niece Keasha and my nephew Lentez, I want to thank you for loving your Aunt and allowing your Aunt to love you. My roommate Trice, who allowed me to be myself and to have that one extra friend to confide in. **I LOVE YOU** girl! To Randy, for staying a true friend to me and not expecting me to be something that I'm not. Thank you for being there for me and for loving my children. **I WILL ALWAYS CHERISH YOU** for that. You are what every woman needs in her life, an honest and real friend! To the one man that has been in my life since I was 8 years old, you know who you are. We have a bond that no one can ever break. I'll **ALWAYS** hold a place for you in my heart! Simply said! Most importantly, thanking the greatest person of all, **I want to thank God for being God alone** and for giving me three beautiful children that is my real inspiration in all that I do. They are the reason that I want to wake up every morning and my reason for accomplishing all that I do and all that I have. **I LOVE YOU WHOLE HEARTEDLY!** My three beautiful children, Parriz, Parrish Jr. and Pediaiah, they have taught me the definition of love and they are the reason for this book entitled:

Sister, Set Yourself Free

CHAPTERS

1) Knowing What Love Is and
   The Meaning Of Love 1

2) Respecting Yourself...9

3) Respect Your Family (Parents, Kids,
   Spouse/Lover & Friends)............................. 19

4) OPEN YOUR EYES! 27

5) Stop Complaining!.. 47

6) BECOMING FREE!...................................... 52

Knowing What Love Is   *Chapter 1*

and

The Meaning Of Love

Does anyone really know what love is? I ask this question because love has been known to have many different definitions. Webster's Dictionary, various other dictionaries, the Holy Bible, scholars and even professors of psychology and sociology can give anyone their definition of love. However, my favorite definition is the Bibles version and the Bible defines love as this: Love is patient. Love is kind. Love is not jealous, it does not brag. Love is not proud. Love is not rude, it is not selfish. Love does not get upset with others. Love does not count the wrongs that has been done. Love is not happy with evil, but is happy with the truth. Love patiently accepts all things. Love always trusts, always hopes, and always remain strong. Love never ends. (1 Corinthians 13:4-9)

Many people do not look at love as a sacred gift. They take love for granted. They say "I Love You" without any real meaning or feelings behind it. A guy I once dated use to tell every woman that he came into contact with for a week or longer that he loved them. He said it so often that it became a simple meaningless statement. True love is one of the greatest gifts in life. It's a gift of endless value. Love is joy, comfort, excitement, hopes, dreams, and most of all security. This is normally where people make their mistake in life, in defining and being in a relationship where they think there is true love.

Everyone, including myself, have been in a relationship where they thought they were experiencing true love. People stay in abusive, controlling relationships, in unfaithful relationships and in unhappy relationships, because they think they are in **LOVE**. They endure all forms of pain, hurt and humiliation (whether known or unknown). They promise to stick by their man or woman even if they are pulling them down and breaking apart every piece of their heart. They believe in their mate and trust him wholeheartedly, while the whole time, he is taking that love that they are sacrificing for granted. I know what that is like because I have been through that personally.

Love **is** about respect: respect for your mind, body, soul and spirit. A man shouldn't ask you to think the way he thinks or to change your looks or appearance or even ask you to compromise your religion for **LOVE.** You are allowed to have your own originality, your own thoughts, your own way of dressing or looking and definitely allowed to continue to worship in your own way. Men are known for saying the classic line "If you love me, then you would do it" or "I love you baby, now is that too much to ask". Don't compromise your inner self for anyone except for yourself.

Love is about trust: trusting your instincts, your heart and trusting each other. You **CAN NOT** have a happy, successful, lasting relationship if there is no trust. You have to be able to believe that your mate is doing the right thing when they are not with you. You can not constantly wonder if they are cheating, lying or trying to deceive you. No matter how hard it seems, you have to believe that they won't break your heart and take advantage of your love for them or else you will only drive yourself crazy wondering what they are doing. Not questioning their actions silently within yourself or aloud doesn't make you dumb, but it allows you to TRUST and that's what everyone wants in a relationship. If it's true love and it's real, then you won't need to question them anyway. You will trust them with every breath you have and it won't be destroyed. Trust is normally given to each other right from the start, however, when people have been hurt in past relationships, they find themselves making people have to earn it from them. When you are fortunate enough to be given trust, cherish it. Cherish it like it's your life. Don't take it for granted. Constantly respect and love the person that is trusting you.

Love **is** about peace: inner peace, outer peace and eternal peace. When you are truly happy in your relationship, you will endure peace. I'm not saying that you won't have arguments or disagreements from time to time, because you will, I'm only saying that you shouldn't be depressed or on the verge of depression due to your relationship. No man or woman should have you crying yourself to sleep or constantly focusing on what they are doing at all times. You should have such a peace that when other people see you, they should see just how happy you two are together. It shouldn't be temporary, but instead, eternal.

When I was married I thought I was in love, but when I look back on that relationship, I realize that it was more of fear than love. Yes, I did **LOVE** my ex-husband, but sometimes people can hurt you so many times and in so many ways that they strip all the love that you have for them away. No matter how many times that he cheated on me or abused me, I thought that my love could change him. Was that stupid or what? I use to believe that one day he would appreciate the wife that he had and the family that we created together and that he would change and love me the way that I loved him, but he never did. Instead, every time that he cheated on me or abused me, he would slowly strip my heart of the love that I carried for him. What I use to consider love turned into fear. It was fear of the next hit or the next phone call from another female that he was sleeping with or had slept with. It wasn't until I started loving myself that I realized that he could never truly love me and me only. Finally, one day I decided that enough was enough and I knew that it was time for me to let go.

It took me some time to realize that everyone is different and every man is different as well. Believe me, this is a true fact even if you don't want to admit it or believe it. I know that at times, they all seem to act the same, but there is that small percentage that is truly genuine. There is that 'right one' as some people say. There is that man or woman that can come along and change your whole point of view and your way of thinking and make you fall in love as if you had never fell in love before. When you think that you have given up on love, cupid shows up and make you feel like a silly little school girl with a crush on the captain of the football team. Yes, you might have been in love once before, but every time is different. What you have to determine is if it is really love or is it infatuation. You have to be able to put the looks, smile, and that personality aside to see what is really there. You have to think with a clear mind and not with your emotions, even if it means taking some time out for yourself.

No one said that love was simple. By all means, love can be complicated, but it doesn't have to remain that way. People say that we can't choose the people that we fall in love with, but I believe otherwise. I believe that you do have the ability to choose who you love. You know if you are dating the towns bad boy or the guy that could be labeled as the Man of the Year. You have to set standards in what you want in a relationship and don't let anyone change those standards. You have to determine if he is right for you and stick to your first instinct. A majority of the time, your first instinct is the right instinct, no matter what you want to believe. My mom use to tell me that you can't always judge a book by its cover, and boy was she right. Although I hated to listen to her at the time, she knew what she was talking about. I've dated the pretty boys, ugly boys, white, black, Indian, and even a half-Mexican, and one thing that I have discovered, is that they are definitely all different. Finding love isn't your responsibility, although people search high and low for it. Love should find you. You have to realize that you are special by all means and that you deserve the best. Don't settle for just anything! Remember this, if you settle now, you'll be settling for the rest of your life.

Respecting Yourself   *Chapter 2*

As I stated earlier, love **is** about respect: respect
for your mind, body, soul and spirit, but it is also about
respecting yourself. How can you love anybody if you
don't respect yourself, both within and on the outside?
You have to know that you control the person that you
are. You control the way you act, dress and look. Some
women today have little respect for themselves. Instead
of looking at their inner beauty, they think that they
have to almost be naked to get attention from men. They
wear the cut off, see through shirts and the "booty"
shorts/skirts to get a reaction from men. I'm not judging
anybody, because I was once guilty of doing the same
thing until I began to respect myself and my body. One

way to know if a man is really interested in you is by being yourself. That means to cover your body and let him see your inner beauty. Show him that you are a real woman in all forms. Let him imagine what's under your clothing, instead of showing him on the first date you're on or the first time that he meets you. Let him appreciate you and most of all respect you.

Most women make that crucial mistake of letting a man sleep with them that first night that they are alone together. Women read this carefully and if you have to, write it down and constantly read it over and over again, **NO MAN RESPECTS A WOMAN THAT HE CAN SLEEP WITH EASILY**, especially if he just met her. I know this for a fact because during a vast majority of my life, I have hung around men and they have all said the same thing about women that are easy to sleep with. When a woman gives her body to a man that easily, she is called 'easy, trash, a tramp, a slut, a whore, and the most familiar word, a ho'. Although he might call her again, it's only for sex and I can almost guarantee you that nine times out of ten, he will never look at you as relationship material. Don't fool yourself and say that you are different, because to him, you're not. You have to realize that if he wanted to really know you, then nothing would interfere with him doing so. Stop thinking that you have to use your body to get what you want, but instead, use your mind. Know that you are worth more than that five minutes or so of sex. Know that you deserve more than to be a mat for that man. Know that you are a beautiful woman in all that you do and in all that you say. Know that you don't and that you won't settle for less in a man. Realize that you deserve to be treated like a queen at **ALL** times.

Being a woman is hard enough, so why would you let a man degrade you or better yet, why do women let men use them? If you truly respected yourself, you would know what a real woman deserves out of life and out of a man. This doesn't mean that you have to be alone forever, but it doesn't hurt to know yourself before you try to know someone else.

A lot of women sleep with numerous men because they have little or no self-respect for themselves. An ex-friend of mine use to sleep with men and say that she slept with them because they made her feel special and said all the right things to her. To me, I thought that she was lacking a little common sense, but then I began to realize that she wasn't the only woman that felt that way. Some women need a man in their life, even if it's only for that five minutes of pleasure in order to feel special or worthy. They constantly need someone to look at them or desire them in order to feel whole. Society blames insecurity and promiscuity on the family or lack of a father, but I blame it on that individual person that is displaying that behavior. No one forces a woman to open her legs to every man that whispers those sweet nothings in her ear, and believe me, that's all it is, sweet nothings. You have to have respect for yourself in order to walk away from Mr. Smooth. You have to be able to know that he's not worth the sacrifice of your self-respect. As my Grandma Annie use to say, "Don't let these little boys/men talk you out of your panties". Yes, it can be hard to say no, but you only have one reputation in life and you should cherish that with every thing you have. Don't let a man or any man convince you that sleeping with him is the best thing for you to do. Instead, convince him that you are more than an easy piece. If you are destined to give it to him, make him work for it. What I mean by that is, make him wait and wonder what it's like to be with you. Let him take you out and wine and dine you for as long as possible. Make him appreciate you and the person you are. Make him know that you are special and beautiful on the inside and on the outside. **Don't**, and I repeat, **don't** let him get it easy!

Respect yourself enough to realize that you can wait for the right man to enter into your life to show him what intimacy is. You can't let every man you're with know every thing that you do in the bedroom. Some women try to turn every man that they are with out. They try to blow their mind with all kinds of things and do all kinds of things in the bed. What these women are failing to realize is that yes, the man may be enjoying it, but I can almost assure you, that he will tell somebody about it the next day. When he thinks of you, he doesn't think of that beautiful, intelligent woman that you are, instead, he thinks of you as that freak that he was with last night or the night before.

If you are a virgin, have faith in the ability that you can wait. It doesn't matter if you are a man or a woman, you need to realize that your first time should be special and with someone who really loves you. I can easily tell you to wait until you are married, but being realistic, most people don't. For some reason, they are ready and willing to loose their virginity to the first person that tells them that they are special. Remember that there are some people out there that don't have your best interest in mind. Not everyone believe in preserving your body for that 'right person' or because it's just the right thing to do. You have to be the smart one that says "No, I can wait". As my girlfriend Mandy always says, "Be true to thine own self".

Respect yourself enough not to continue to be with a man that you know that lives with his woman. Men are known for living with their woman and still dating other people as well. They are quick to claim that they are so unhappy at home or that their girlfriend has mental problems, however, when they are caught cheating, they go back to that "psycho girlfriend". Now explain that one to me! If that man wanted to be with you, when he is caught cheating, he will let his girlfriend know that he is "so" unhappy and that he wants to be with you. If he goes back to his woman, then you need to realize that all you were to him was a "booty-call" no matter what he says. He will try to make you believe that he really cares for you, but don't buy into that act. Honestly, that's all it is, an "**ACT**"! First of all, if he loved her, he wouldn't hurt her, and if he loved you, he wouldn't try everything in his power to make his girlfriend believe that you don't mean anything to him. He would end his relationship with his girlfriend and explore the possibilities of what the two of you could actually have together. However, why would you want a man that you obtained because he was caught cheating on his woman? If he did it to her, don't you think that he would probably do it to you? Why would you want to take that risk? What that man does with you when the two of you are intimate, you can almost assure yourself that he is doing the same thing to his woman, if not more. Wouldn't you want someone that you could almost guarantee that was with you and only with you? Don't allow yourself to be played like a violin, easy and smooth.

If you are the one that is being cheated on and you catch him cheating with another woman, don't be disrespectful and curse that woman out, maintain your position as a woman, and remain ladylike. Don't call her all kinds of names and make yourself look dumb, besides, he is the one that lays beside you at night and tells you that he loves you. Hate him, not her! It doesn't matter if she knew that he had a woman or not, he is the one that is responsible for breaking your heart. If he continues to cheat, find yourself someone that can appreciate you and that won't hurt you. There are a few men out there that knows how to treat a lady.

Respect yourself enough to not give your partner ultimatums. Never tell your woman or your man that they have to choose between you and their children, you and their employment, or settling down or losing you. Although this may work from time to time, sometimes the outcome may not be what you expect. Some people may not really want to settle down, but at the same rate, they don't want to lose you either. Decisions and all choices for the future should be made mutual without ultimatums. If you force your mate to choose, you will never know what they actually wanted in their life and in due time, not only may it cause problems for your relationship, but your mate may begin to resent you.

Respect yourself enough not to date married men. Although people date married men every day, you should be the one to take the stand to say "NO". When I was married, a smart man once told a woman that was sleeping with my husband that if he really wanted you, then he would leave his wife for you instead of creeping when his wife wasn't around. That same man later told me that if a man truly loves you, especially if you are married, then nothing would make him cheat. Now that I am divorced, I know that he was only telling her and I the truth. Dating married men is a choice, it doesn't matter if you believe that it is right or wrong, it's still a choice. **DON'T** be a convenience for that man, but if you do decide to do it anyway, make it worth your time. Don't just sleep with that man, make him wine you and dine you as well. Make him pay **your** bills and take care of **you** the same way that he takes care of his wife. If he is smothering her in diamonds, don't settle for cubic zurconians, instead demand diamonds too. Requiring things in a relationship doesn't make you easy or better yet, a "gold digger", but it does let him know that this ride isn't for free. Don't let him trick you into believing that he is doing you a favor by seeing you and definitely don't let him think that he has the upper hand. Make him realize that you don't need him, but that he needs you. Make him think about you all the time and want you when you aren't around. Make him believe that you are the best thing that has ever happened to him. Some people believe that if you are going to date a married man, then you should do it with a conscience, but you have to realize that what goes around comes around, or better yet, you reap what you sow.

Respect Your Family   *Chapter 3*
(Parents, Kids, Spouse/Lover & Friends)

The best way to respect yourself is by respecting your family, children, spouse/lover, and your friends. When you respect your family, you show them that you appreciate and love them. People often believe that they can do whatever they choose and it won't affect their family and their love one's, but they're wrong. Everything that you do or say impact those around you. My Pastor, Pastor Shirley Johnson, use to tell me that power is in the words of the tongue, and you know what, she was right. In other words, every time that you speak negatively about someone you love , you are speaking harm to them or basically putting a curse on their life. At moments when you want to fly off the handle and say the first thing that's on your mind, that's when you need to stop and think first.

As a single, divorced mother of three, I have learned that you have to watch your every action and that you have to respect all people around you. I didn't say that you had to like everyone, I'm just stating that you should respect them. It bothers me to see women who are mothers, acting like they have no children. They club, drink, get high and party all weekend and some during the week, while other people are taking care of their children. When these mothers are home with their children, they don't spend any quality time with them, instead, they turn the television on and let the media entertain their kids and do the job that they are suppose to be doing.. As the children grow up, they rebel against their own mother and have little respect for her. This cycle can be broken if women would only do what they are suppose to do as mothers and as role models. **Women, please, please, please, don't use the excuse that you are a single parent. SO WHAT!** It doesn't matter if you are a single mom. There are plenty of women that raise smart and successful children. For as long as I can remember, women have been raising kids alone. Does being a single parent give you the excuse to sleep with every man you see? Does it allow you to leave your kids at every body else's house so that you can party all night long? Does it give you the excuse to not take responsibility for your own child or children? **NO!** Being a parent is another great gift that you were blessed to have. Respect yourself and your family enough to be that outstanding mother and sole provider. **DON'T** try to wear your children's clothing and think that you look good in it. **DON'T** embarrass your child and yourself. Love yourself enough to know that you look good in your own clothing.

Being a single parent of girls can be difficult at times, but remember that you are the parent. **DON'T** forget that that little girl is **your** daughter, not your best friend. There is nothing wrong with spending a "girl's night out" with your daughter or riding out and talking with her from time to time, but always keep that line between the two of you. Never treat your pre-teen or teenage daughter like an adult, because when you do, she will act like one. She will do things that "adults" do and behave like "adults" do. When you talk to her, leave out the details from your night out. When you are shopping for personal (sexy) clothing, let her go to another department in the store or simply leave her at home. Don't buy clothes for her that makes her look older than she really is. Your job is protect her and teach her how to be a lady, not a female on the street. Keep her in clothing that covers her body, but still shows her beauty. Also, after you have the "birds and the bees" conversation with her, let it go. Don't make the mistake of trying to include her in "your" personal life. You shouldn't want your daughter to grow up any faster than she has to. If you push your daughter in the wrong direction, she will react and you will only have yourself to blame.

Be a mom, not a warden! Don't be an over-bearing parent!

Parents, get to know your child's friends and the people that they hang out with. It's good for a parent to be protective, but don't be over-bearing. Mothers sometimes forget that they were once teenagers, no matter how many years ago it was. The older their child gets, the stricter the parent becomes. Many mothers make the mistake of telling their teenage child who they can or can't date or be friends with. As a mother, I understand where they are coming from, but as a woman that once received my mothers approval or disapproval's, I totally disagree. Telling your child not to befriend someone because you don't like them, only makes them want to be around that person even more. You should voice your opinion to your teenager about how you feel about that "friend" and why you feel that way, but don't tell them not to befriend them. In time, they will eventually realize that you are right, and for some that may be the same day, while for others it may take a while.

A parents daughter and the men that they date is a bigger, yet ongoing controversy. Most parents still pray for a good man to enter their daughter's life even after their daughter is grown. I know that all mothers want the best for their daughter, but telling her to leave her man alone because you don't approve of him is definitely the wrong way to approach the situation, even if you do think that is for her own good.. Trying to tare her from the man that she **think** she's in love with is only going to drive and push her deeper into his arms. Again, express your feelings to your daughter about that man and let her know why you feel that way, but after that, let her make her final decision. Yes, it is her heart and her life no matter what age she is. Telling her to move on is like telling a deer to move out of the road, it won't happen until she realizes that either her heart or her life is in danger. Life is hard enough for your daughter, as she will learn, so be supportive of her and pray and believe that she will make the right choices without mommy making them for her all the time. Talk to her routinely and get to know the young lady that she is forming into. Don't allow her "peers" to be her support group. You are, can be, and probably is the only most important role model in your child's life, but you have to be objective sometimes. Everything you do and say will place an impact on your child's life, especially during those critical pre-teen and teenage years. It's important for them to know that they can depend on you when they need advice or just an open ear. There are so many girls running away from home or turning to prostitution because of lack of love, attention, or both at home. Love your child unconditionally and most of all listen to her. Let her know and be assured that you are always there for her and that you are available for her anytime day or night. Remember that God holds you accountable for the children that he blessed you to have. Put your children first and never let any relationship that you are in come before them.

Finally, respect your children enough to not talk negatively about their other parent. When you are raising your child or children alone, and the absent parent is never around, you do get frustrated. There are times that you probably will think and say resentful things about them, but don't express those opinions to your child. No matter how sorry the other parent is, that is your child's mom or dad. To them, the parent that is rarely a part of their life is like gold to them. Your feelings for them are not their feelings for their parent. Don't try to turn them against them. As your child grow up, they will understand and realize how you were the only one their for them and they will respect you even more for not disrespecting their mom or dad.

OPEN YOUR EYES!   *Chapter 4*

If you noticed, I capitalized the title in this chapter because this chapter is very important to me and should be for **ALL** women! If you were drowning in a relationship before you read this book or when you began reading this book, then you should be at the awakening point in your life by now, if not, then hopefully you will be when you are done reading this chapter or this book.

While contemplating what to say in this chapter, I knew that it was definitely for women to know but for men to understand and know as well! I want everyone who reads this book to open their eyes and evaluate the situation or situations that they are in at this very moment. Before you read any further, take a few seconds and meditate on everything that you have been through in your relationship now and in past relationships and then stop and evaluate where you are right now. Do you see where things went wrong and how some of those situations could have been prevented? Good! Now stop. Stop making excuses for that man or that woman and open your eyes. You can't change the past, but you can definitely change the present and shape the future. Personally in my life and in dealing with relationships, I like to refer to a scripture that is in the Bible and it reads "God, grant me the serenity to accept the things that I cannot change, the courage to change the things that I can, and the wisdom to know the difference". Every time that I read or hear that Biblical verse, it helps me to overcome situations that I am going through now.

Opening your eyes can be related to so many things. It can relate to being in an unhappy employment position, partnership, friendship, relationship, or even an unhappy marriage. People stay in unhappy jobs because they are comfortable there or because they have been there for many years. You can have the same position for years and maybe the same pay or a smaller increase in pay, but you aren't happy, only content. Some people feel that they can't get a better job or go back to school, but at times like that, you need to realize that you can. You need to place a goal for yourself and hold firm to it. It doesn't matter if it takes years to accomplish that goal, believe that you can do it and don't let anyone or anything stand in your way.

Open your eyes can mean opening your eyes to deceiving, back-stabbing friends. My sister, Laticiama always told me that you can't trust everyone that smiles and calls themselves your friend. After being betrayed twice by other so-called female friends, I finally realized that she was right and became determined that I **WILL NOT** be betrayed a third time. Some women can be so scandalous that it makes you think twice about befriending women all together. Don't get me wrong, men do the same thing. I have seen two men that were best friends and they have slept with each others women before too. I guess you can say that now days you can't put your trust in every body. I have a female roommate that I am fortunate enough to trust with my life, but recently I experienced a situation when I wasn't as fortunate. I allowed a friend of hers to come and live with us to help her out and she betrayed me for weeks without me knowing it. I was buying this friend clothes, taking her out to eat, helped her find a job, really befriending her and trying to put her in my "sister" category, but soon came to realize that she was stabbing me in my back while smiling in my face. I discovered that she was seeing a close male friend of mine. Was I mad when I found out? What do you think? I had my suspicions all along that they were seeing each other when I was at work or just wasn't around, but it wasn't until my roommate confirmed that it was true that I had to face the situation head on. Yes, I was heated and reacted to those emotions by taking it out on her, but she was wrong. I do feel bad sometimes about some of the things that I said to her, but if the shoe was on the other foot, she probably would had reacted the same way that I did. I guess I felt more betrayed by her than him. He wasn't my boyfriend or someone that I was committed to, but we had dated and were still seeing each other from time to time. I wasn't ready for anything serious with him at the moment and I felt like he wasn't really ready either and boy was my instincts right. However, she knew what we had and that we were still dating and she still chose to see him without my consent and behind my back. I do however know that a man will be a man. If a woman is offering a man sexual favors or offering to be intimate with him without telling the other woman, nine times out of ten, he is going to do it. Believe me, he **WILL** take her up on that offer. Anyway, back to that roommate, she had a son and I wanted to help her out so badly that I didn't listen to people back home when they advised me not to let her move in, but I had to learn the hard way and that lesson was that you can't help everyone. A majority of my life, I've always had the problem of trying to be everyone's life raft without worrying about if they were going to pull me under while I was trying to save them. There has been a few people that has tried hard to pull me down. I have and was trying so hard to be there for them, but do you know who was there to rescue me besides my mom and oldest sister, when others began to pull me under? I can tell you, NO

ONE! I always had to be strong enough to pull myself up from drowning. I've always had to be my own life raft. I never had that person in my life to tell me that it was okay and that they would help me through this situation. Sometimes, it is a bad feeling, but at times, I'm grateful to know that God has made me strong enough to move on. I'm not mad at her anymore, maybe still a little hurt, but definitely not mad. Life can throw you so many obstacles, but you just have to learn how to duck and roll. Don't let people who are out to hurt you or destroy you, see you hurting or down. No matter how hard it is, suck it up and every time you see them, smile and let them know that they didn't destroy you. I am a firm believer in the saying that "Kindness kills". I know that sometimes, even when you don't want to or think that you have the strength to be kind, you have to turn the other cheek and do just that. I'm not telling you to be a fool or anyone's door mat, but don't let people get you down. Remember that what don't kill you will only make you stronger. Life is way too short to be stressing yourself over that man or that woman that doesn't appreciate the person that you are or that "so-called" friend that betrayed you and didn't appreciate or value the meaning of friendship. What one person misses out on or take advantage of is another person fortune.

Relationships can blind you and make you temporarily stupid if you are not careful. It amazes me how everyone around you can see how that man or woman is no good for you, but you think that they are made out of gold. You are constantly explaining yourself, arguing, fighting, cheating, and even saying harmful things to one another, but you're still saying and thinking that you're in love. Everyone else around you can see that you deserve better, but you think that you have the best. I believe that we all have been there before, and the sad thing about it is that some people are there now. Destiny's Child said it best in track #7 called "Bad Habit" of their new CD, Destiny Fulfilled. I have played that track often for a close friend of mine while praying that she was paying attention to the words. You can probably name a few people right now that you think are with the wrong person. One thing that I have discovered is that you can't tell someone who thinks that they are in love to let go of their mate. Doing that can not only make you lose a friend and push them closer to their mate. As hard as it is to stand by and let someone you love or care about be deceived, you have to keep quiet and let them learn on their own. One thing that I have learned by experience is that sometimes the hardest lessons learned are those that hurt.

Open your eyes to cheaters. There are couples that cheat on their mate everyday in America. There are several signs that indicates if your mate is cheating on you and all of them are noticeable if you would only open your eyes. These are 10 of the many ways to tell if you have an unfaithful mate:

1) They come home from a night of being out with friends and go straight to the shower.

2) When the cell phone rings, they grab it quickly whether you were going to answer it or not.

3) They hide or sleep with their cell phone at night.

4) Every time your phone rings and you answer it, the caller hangs up when you say hello.

5) They begin to buy condoms on the regular or the condoms that they already have starts disappearing.

6) They buy more cologne or perfume and becomes more obsessed about the way they look when they leave the house.

7) They begin to spend more time away from you and home.

8) They always have to go out of town and their work pay becomes less and unaccounted for.

9) They start becoming uninterested or less interested in intimacy with you.

10) When you are intimate with one another, they get up as soon as they are finished.

There are other ways to tell if you have an unfaithful mate, but if you answered yes to any one of the 10 listed signs, then you need to open your eyes and move on. You can call me crazy, but for all the people who have been cheated on before or is being cheated on now, think about numbers 1-10. Have your mate or is your mate showing any of those signs? Some people believe in the saying, "Once a cheater, always a cheater", but

I don't. There was a time when I did believe in that saying, but I know that sometimes you can actually cheat on a person, and when you realize how bad you have hurt them, you vow and hold to the fact that you won't do it again. Cheating can have such a great impact and outcome on the person that was cheated on. Either way, don't punish yourself and think that it's your fault that you're being cheated on no matter what they says. Being in love doesn't mean that you have to be a fool. Be strong and take your life and your heart back.

Open your eyes to the user. If a man only calls you when he is horny, cut him lose. Don't fall for the line that he has been working all day or that he thought about you, but he didn't have time to call. If he wanted to make time for you, he could have no matter what was going on around him. Don't give any man the notion that he can call you any time during the night and you will let him in or go out to meet him. If you are unsure about if sex is all he wants from you, then simply ask him or get creative with how you ask him and set him up for the question. Ask him how does he feel about the two of you in a relationship, even if you are not ready for one, or better yet, ask him out on a date. If he answers no to either question or makes up an excuse, then you know that he is only interested in sex with you. However, if you are going to be a "booty-call" girl/ woman, set limitations. If you're working, in school, or have children, let that man know that he can' t call after 10 p.m. or so. If you always make yourself available when he calls, then you are letting him know that you are always available for him.

Open your eyes to "runners". Today there are so many people that are afraid to settle down with one person, and because of this fear, they run from relationship to relationship. Both men and women are guilty of running. Some women run because they have been hurt in previous relationships and they are afraid that it will happen again. Most men run because they are simply afraid of commitment, and because commitment means change. Men want to have their cake a eat it too. I have known men to have a wonderful, honest, caring female in their life and they refuse to settle down with that female. To some men, settling down means losing their freedom instead of gaining a partner in life. If a man tells you that he's into you but he can't settle down right now because he's been hurt or because he needs to get some things straight in his life before he settles down, then he's just running games on you. Nine times out of ten, what he's really saying to you is, "Baby, I think you are fine and I like sleeping with you, but I don't want any commitments right now. However, I still want to see you and sleep with you, but I want to see other people as well". Ladies, when you hear this, tell that man where to go and how to get there. Don't let that man continue to disrespect you and waste your time. Let him know that you deserve a better man in your life.

Open your eyes to dead beats. When I say dead beats, I am referring to the father of your child or that man that won't get a job. In today's society, there is no excuse for any man to be unemployed. My mom always said that if a man wanted to work, then he would rake leaves or cut grass if he had to in order to take care of his family. No man should be depending on any woman to care of him. I understand that a man can and does go through hard times every now and then, and in those circumstances, there is an exception to the rule. If your man gets sick or laid off from his job, then yes, by all means, support your man until he gets back on his feet. Let him know that you have his back. Be his crutch, but don't be his wheel chair. Don't carry this man forever. There are so many women that allow their man to be unemployed and live with them. These women have steady jobs, their own house and most of the time, their own vehicle, and instead of their man supporting them or at least meeting them half way, these women are supporting their man. To me, there is definitely something wrong with that picture. How can a man call himself a man when he doesn't even have a job? He sits at home all day doing nothing, drinking, or getting high while his woman is out working and taking care of him. Then when she gets home, he wants to know what she is cooking for dinner instead of him having dinner ready for her. What's sad about the whole situation is that women allow this to happen! They cater to a man that should be called a boy or better yet, a dead beat. I know plenty of women that have men living with them and they are taking care of him. These women are smart, pretty, intelligent, and probably could have any man they want, but they choose to be with the sorriest man that they can find. These men that they are with can't even pay the light bill for them or baby-sit the children while they work. It doesn't take a brain surgeon to know that these men are only using these women. All he wants is a place to lay his head and call home, and like fools, some women provide that atmosphere for them. I have been that fool before in my life, but when I opened my eyes and realized that I was only being used and taking advantage of, I had to let that man go. I knew within myself that I was too good to be used. Once again I am telling you to realize that you deserve better and that you are no body's door mat.

Being a dead beat by not taking care of your child is ridiculous. If a man helped a woman to create a child, then why should someone else make him take care of that child by paying child support. There wasn't a judge or lawyer in the bed when the two of you were creating it. Having to put a man on child support is embarrassing not only for you and him, but for that child as well. No child wants to grow up and know that their parent had to be forced to take care of them. Women, if your child's father doesn't want to be a man and take care of his responsibility, then don't push the issue. If you have already put him on child support, let it go. If he doesn't pay, don't call the child support office every week until he gets locked up. When your child grows up, they'll know and remember who was there for them. Remember, what goes around comes around. No one can do someone wrong and live a wonderful life. Life will make sure that they pay one way or another. Just know that you can be a great mother and a father alone. My mother did it and now so am I, so I know that it is possible. Never think that you can't do it alone.

Open your eyes to relationships that are together only for the children's sake. People have been known to rush into committed relationships because they are expecting a child with their partner. Having a child before marriage is Biblically wrong, but it this is another situation that happens everyday. Women become mothers and men become fathers and a majority of the time, the first thing they do is either get married or move in together. They want to do the right thing and have good intentions in the beginning, but when they really get to know each other and how the other person lives and really is, then they realize that they weren't really in love. Now after the "honeymoon" stage is gone, they want out. They begin to ask themselves why. First of all, getting married or moving in together because you are expecting a child is the wrong thing to do. You are not only hurting yourself, but the child as well. If you aren't marrying or making the decision to live together for true love, then open your eyes and realize that you can be a great parent alone and without rushing into something that can be even harder to get out of. Men, you can be a great dad without rushing into another situation as well. Whatever you choose, do it with your eyes open, weigh out all your options, have a clear conscious, and know if it's for love or for guilt.

Open your eyes to marriage. People have been known for staying in unhappy marriages because it's convenient. I've seen married people so unhappy and treat each other with little or no respect, but refuse to let go. I would never suggest to anyone to leave their spouse, unless they were being abused or constantly cheated on, but I think that a peace of mind is as valuable as it gets. Why would you let your mate talk to you any way that they choose to and why would you stay in a situation that you weren't happy in? Happiness is one of the keys to success. I have witnesses people go to work and enjoy their day, and then dread the time when they have to go home to their mate. To me, that's crazy. Happiness is essential for both work and home. When you're unhappy at home, but you love your mate, talk to them about how you feel, go to counseling, do all you can to make it work and don't give up so easily. There are so many couples in America getting divorced daily, so don't add to the statistics. You have to live with the fact of knowing if you gave it all you had or if you just took the easy road out. . Exhaust all your options before making any final decisions.

Open your eyes to violent relationships. Remaining in an domestic violence situation is also another topic that needs and has to be addressed. In a past relationship, I was once that battered woman, so I know what I am talking about. Being battered is like living in constant fear, fear for your life and fear for the life of your family.

You have to constantly wonder if he's going to be angry at you or hit you today for something you said or did. You have to dress, act, think, say and even react the way that he wants you to in order to avoid being abused. Sometimes it may work, but at other times, no matter what you say or do, he will still abuse you.

Fear is a form of control. When a spouse or mate has you living in fear of them, then they have the control. When they have conquered control over your entire body, they focus on your mentality. They want control over your life, your thoughts, your emotions and even your spirit and mind. They try to destroy you piece by piece and force you to believe that you are nothing without them. It's the control that makes them feel important or superior.

Domestic Violence has an awareness month once a year. It's a time to remember all the women that has been beaten or abused. However, awareness should be made every month. Being battered and surviving it requires great strength. No one can truly relate to a battered woman except for a survived battered woman. I know that many psychologists and counselors are educationally able to console women that are living in domestic violence situations, but until you have been through it yourself, you will never really be able to relate or understand. Children grow up every day with parents who batter the other parent. They become scared when their parents begin arguing and they conceal their family's problems. They begin to live in fear and then the cycle begins.

My children suffered in an abusive home. Even though I was being battered, I tried to make it work and at times it did, but the change was not genuine. The battering continued and my children were paying the real costs. When my son began to react to his dad's behavior and began to be too aggressive and my oldest daughter began crying when my sister and I would wrestle with one another, I knew that they were being affected and scarred. I knew that I had to make some quick decisions for their sake. I knew that I had to leave and never look back.

Children learn from what they see and when they see their father abusing their mother, they think it's okay to be an abuser or be abused when they get older. Battered parents need to think of not only their life, but the life that God entrusted for them to care for. Simply put, GET OUT!!!!!! If you have children, let them know that battering isn't acceptable and that they shouldn't batter either. Help them to heal any scares that were created during your relationship. Let your children know that you are putting them first now and that they can live in a peaceful home. Give them that security that they need to have. Let them know that you will protect them at all costs. If you have to , go to a shelter, friends, family or even a neighbors, but get out! Know and believe that you can have a partner that won't hit you or abuse you. Know that you deserve to be treated with respect and don't settle for anything less. Build confidence in your self that will allow you to remain strong and pray that God gives you the strength to continue to be strong. This doesn't mean that you have to stop loving your spouse or mate, but it does mean that you can move on. If you want them back, wait until they get professional help and show a genuine change. For your own sake and the sake of your life, open your eyes to life and to living it without fear.

Stop Complaining!   *Chapter 5*

There are a number of reason that people complain about their mate, however, constant complaining can break-up a relationship easily. If you are going to stay in your relationship with your mate, stop complaining to everyone about them. Instead of complaining about all the things that are wrong with them, begin complimenting the things that are right. No one wants to be with a complaining partner.

Ladies and gentlemen hear this, if you have someone that is a hard worker, going to school and want the finer things in life, support them and stop complaining when they are working all the time or going to school. You can't have it both ways. For some reason, some people actually complain when their mate has a real job and is out being the bread winner. Can you believe that? You can't expect you mate to spend that quality time that **YOU** want if you are expecting them to take care of you. You have to make some sacrifices in life order to obtain your dreams. Some people say that they want a good mate, but when they have that, they don't know how to appreciate it. They begin to find the smallest things to complain about. They complain about them snoring too loud or waking up in the middle of the night for a drink of water. Whatever they can find wrong with them, they find it. I guess after you have been in so many bad relationships, it's hard to adjust to the good ones. Instead of trying to find fault in the mate that you have now, appreciate them.

Every woman wants an honest and committed man. Women are hard enough to live with as is, so if you are fortunate enough to have a good man that come home to you, love him! Let him know every day that you are happy to have him as your man. Before he leaves the house in the morning, let him know that you love him. When he comes home from work, have dinner ready and waiting. When you are both in the bed at night, hold him or let him hold you. Tell him that you love him again when you say goodnight. Before you go to sleep, thank God for sending him your way and for placing him in your life. Let him know that he is loved and constantly reassure him of that. **NEVER, and I repeat, NEVER** go to bed angry! If you get into an argument during the day, apologize before you go to bed at night. It doesn't matter who was right or wrong, have peace in your home. Kiss him good-bye every time he leaves your presence. Always cherish, love, adore and support your man in all that he does and is doing. Let him know that you have his back and that you are in his corner at all times.

If you have a man that comes home to you every night and is not out in the streets with his friends and other women, be thankful. Don't complain if he wants to go out with his friends at least one night out the week. Once again, you have to trust that he is doing the right thing. If you doubt him and complain all the time, you will only push him the opposite direction. Sometimes complaining to your mate does work, but you have to remember that they are not going to change until they are ready to do so. Your complaining isn't making him do it any faster.

Every man wants a faithful and loving woman. Women, again, don't degrade yourself by sleeping with every man that says you're cute. No man wants to turn a "ho" into a house wife. Men, if you are fortunate enough to have a woman that can put up with you and love you, then respect her and treat her like gold. Don't complain when she wants you to spend time with her, just do it. There are some women that you have to track down all the time, but if you are blessed enough to have a woman that is waiting at home for you, appreciate it and love her. At night, reassure her that you love her and let her know that you will always be there for her. Be her man and not her father, and if she wants to go back to school, stand behind her and support her in her goals and dreams.

If you are a mother with kids and you find a man that wants to be there for you and those kids, hold on to him tight. I always tell people that I am a packaged deal, when you buy one, you get three free. There are so many men that are afraid to be fill-in fathers, but for those that do step up to the plate, it takes guts. If you have a mate that treats your child or children like his own, then respect him and make sure that your children respect him as well. Not everyone can be a father to someone else's kids and love them as if they were their own and not every woman can do the same either. It takes an unselfish and courageous person to do that. It requires unconditional love that is beyond measures.

BECOMING FREE!   *Chapter 6*

Now that you are almost finished reading this book, you should be on the way to setting yourself free. Being free from a bad situation is a wonderful experience. It's like being locked up in jail or prison and finally being allowed to go home. It's hard being in a relationship, so why would anyone want to be held in relationship bondage.

Being free in mind, spirit, body and soul is so essential to not only your physical well being, but for your emotional well being as well. Relationships requires time, strength, courage, faith and unconditional love. Couples would interact and respond to one another better once they realize that they have to trust and be honest with their mate first and love them like they want to be loved. Relationships does require change, but when you are in a relationship, you can not change the person that are with. In order for someone to change, they have to want to do so on their own. Any change should be genuine, not forced.

Being in love requires ultimate trust. Trust is such a valuable commodity within any relationship. A relationship without trust is like a house without windows, after a while, you feel trapped and suffocated and you want out. You have to and need to trust your partner and have faith in the love that they have for you.

Love is an emotion that should never be taken for granted. A friend of mine is always telling me that he loves the mother of his son wholeheartedly, however, he is always cheating on her. His excuse for the reason that he does what he do is because they are temporarily broken-up. Excuse my language, but I see it as bull-crap. As I constantly state, love requires respect for yourself and respect for one another. You can not and do not love your partner if you are cheating on them.

The young lady that the friend of mine is still seeing is the lady that he once cheated on his girlfriend with. Although he claims to no longer be in a relationship, I know that if his ex-girlfriend (son's mother) knew that he was still seeing the other woman, she would go crazy. Although I know that he cares dearly for his son's mother, I don't believe that he is in love with her. When you love someone, you **have to** put yourself in the other person's shoes. If his ex-girlfriend had cheated on him while they were together and it caused them to break-up, he would be mad if he found out that she was still seeing the man that she cheated with, especially if she was still telling him that she loved him when he would come to see his son. No matter how much he tries to convince himself, there is no way that he could truly love her. When you love someone, you will never do anything intentional to hurt them and by him still seeing the other woman, if his son's mom found out, she would be hurt because the pain would resurface of how he betrayed her by seeing that woman. Unfortunately, I know that there is nothing worst in a relationship than reliving a painful situation.

In the past, I have given my share of hurt in relationships and I have definitely received more than my share, and during this process, I have learned that a heart should never be played with. When a woman feels betrayed, there is always that possibility that she will seek revenge. When a woman is scorned, the payback can be unimaginable.

The heart is so fragile and carries many emotions. It is hard to repair any emotional damages that has been done to it. If you have been given the entrance and acceptance into one's heart, embrace it. There are so many people that wants love and acceptance from another individual. They wish that they could have someone to come home to every night and someone that they can say "I love you" to. If you have that special someone in your life, treasure every moment and thank God that he allowed for it to be.

Becoming free is not difficult to accomplish. You just have to realize that you are special and deserve to be treated that way. You should never allow any woman or man to physically abuse you, mentally abuse you, cheat on you, disgrace you, disrespect you or treat you less than a queen or a king. You have to set standards for yourself and stick to those standards. If you comprise any of your standards, then you will be compromising your heart as well. However, any compromise that you do make has to be mutual between you and your mate. It has to be willing, without any second thoughts or hesitations to do it.

Love should not be about controlling the person that you are with, but instead it should be about becoming one and supporting them in all that they do. Truly loving someone and having someone to love you is an experience beyond measures. It can set you free from past painful relationships and open up doors that you thought would never be open again.

Never let one bad relationship keep you from opening your heart back up to another one. Never let anyone hold you back from being the man or woman that you want to be. Never let anyone treat you less than the best and never allow yourself to be used by anyone.

Being free is only as hard as you allow it to be. Know and understand what true love is, respect yourself, respect your family, approach all situations with your eyes open, stop complaining and allow yourself to become and remain free. Remember that people will only treat you the way that you allow them to treat you.

Again, in the words of my favorite scripture:

"God grant me the serenity to accept the things I can not change, the courage to change the things I can and the wisdom to know the difference".

Once you love yourself, you will be able to love others and then you will be able to **SET YOURSELF FREE!**

About the Author

I have always dreamed of being an author since I was a child. However, when I first decided to write a book it was during the downfall of my marriage. I was a mother of three children and on the verge of accomplishing my bachelor's degree. I was going through so much emotionally that I knew that if I began to write down my feelings, I would be able to express myself better and release a lot of pain. When you love someone and dedicate your life to them, you never think that it could end, but when it does it's painful. I have learned a lot over the years about love, pain, surviving alone and knowing what true love is. Now that I have completed this book, not only am I completely free, but I was able to love again.